Finding Me!

Annette T Murray

ISBN: 978-1-7349439-1-7

Library of Congress Cataloging-in-Publication Date is available.

Project Specialist/Author Coach

Barlow Enterprises, LLC

Executive Aspiring Authors Program

Write Your Book Now! Visit: www.destinystatement.com or

Text 478-227-5692

Legal Disclaimer

Ordering Information

Finding Me may be purchased in large quantities at a discount for educational, business, or sales promotional use. For more information or to request Mrs. Annette Murray as the speaker at your next event email: anniemurray05@gmail.com

This book is dedicated to my loving and amazing husband, Johnnie Murray, Jr. You have consistently supported my vision to write my book and to share my story. I'm thankful to have you as my covering for almost thirty years of marriage.

This book is also dedicated to my beloved, late mother, Jacqueline Wiley and to my father, Larry Wiley.

Not least of all, I dedicate this book to my twin sister, Antoinette Tracey and to her husband, Damon Harris; to Ambria Harris, Allenda Burrows, Derek Powell Murray and to the entire Murray, Scott, and Wiley families.

Finally, I dedicate *Finding Me* to my nieces, nephews, and godchildren.

ACKNOWLEDGEMENTS

To my amazing husband who has believed in me from the very beginning, I cannot thank you enough for your love and support. I love you. I am so thankful that God put us together.

There were so many people who have played an intricate part in helping me to write and publish this book. Each of you have played a major role in my healing process. You guided me as I walked through this journey. It has taken me years. You have helped capture some life-changing circumstances, so that I can help encourage others. I could not have done it without you.

Bishop Joseph Scott, Jr. and Lady Marie Scott, Bishop Brenda Cuthbertson, Elder Fred Cuthbertson, Bishop T.D. Jakes, First Lady Serita Jakes, Pastor Cheryl Brady, Maxine Ross, Mercedes Robinson, Claudette Holt, Verdell Osborne and Lynn Stacy Hixon. Thank you!

Finally, I offer heartfelt thanks to my pastors, Bob and Niki Roberts; Pastor Scott; Ashley Venable; and the Northwood Church Family for your love and support.

FOREWORD

John ferociously preached the baptism that was the bridge for repentance of sin. Thousands gathered, on a daily basis, seeking this life-altering message of change. As intrigued as the people were with the relentlessness of John's ministry, and as impressed as John was with the great gathering of seekers, he never forgot, that he was only preparing the way for the one—the one who would bring a baptism that had not been experienced by the world. John knew that he was only preparing the people for the one man who would offer them the baptism of the Spirit.

Jesus arrived at the Jordan River knowing that He *was* the one, all while fully embracing the challenges that He would have to face. Nevertheless, not one of the challenges that we see Jesus endure in scripture had the authority to destroy Him. These challenges would in fact merely ensure that this world-changer would have what He needed to do the miraculous.

What Jesus needed most was not a garrison of soldiers or a parade to acknowledge his awaited presence. What He needed most is exactly what Annette Murray gives to you through this brilliant work, *Finding Me*, and that is the gift of possessing *extreme self-awareness*. This brand of awareness is always birthed by the force of a voice. For Jesus, this voice was heard when the earth was infiltrated with a sound that had not been heard until God the Father declared from the heavens, *"This is my son!"*

That was the moment in which Jesus' earthly ministry was birthed. Embracing the message of this impactful book, *Finding Me*, is your moment!

Annette Murray not only urges us to find ourselves but she takes time to set out strategic patterns of thinking and behaving that will begin a cycle of victory in your life. A strategy is not the only blessing that you receive from reading this book. Annette opens her heart and becomes transparent about her journey! Thus, *Finding Me* is born of experiences, transitions, successes, failures, tearing down, and rebuilding. *Finding Me* exemplifies a life of sacrifice, perplexity, and the redemption of purpose. Doubtless, her writing is inspired by God. Annette's hand is used to pen a story—her story—that serves as a map to freedom for us all.

Welcome to your moment!

Christian Winters

Founder

Influencers International, Inc.

INTRODUCTION

Finding Me was written from a place of deep hurt and pain. Not knowing how to love myself after facing so many challenges in life, eventually caused me to spiral into a dark place. Like many young women, I dreamed. I had plans for my life. I'd honestly hoped that everything would be perfect. Little did I know, although it is not what I planned, there would be hills, valleys, mountains and storms that I would have to walk through. I suffered countless challenges from birth to the age of fifty-one, because I did not realize who I was – until now.

To help you to confront, reflect upon and process some of the hurt and pain that you are working through or have had to deal with in your life, in each of the chapters you will see "Finding Me Reflections," as well as scriptures that brought me great peace during the extremely trying times in my life. As you read, make time to pause and think about the questions in those sections. You can write your responses in your book, so that you can revisit them later and celebrate your growth. I am sure that you will find, as I have, that reflecting, meditating on the scriptures, and writing are also powerful instruments of healing.

Let me share my journey with you.

Annie

Contents

O Lord, you have searched
me and you know me.

Psalm 119:11

My Dream

Keep your heart open to dreams. For as long as there's a dream, there is hope, and as long as there is hope, there is joy in living.

— Anonymous

As a little girl, I always talked about what I wanted to be when I grew up. I already had everything mapped out in my mind. I imagined what my life would look like when I became an adult. I wanted to be a nurse, like my mom. I wanted to get married and have three children. I hoped to do many things in life. I just did not know that life would have so many challenges that I'd have to face, in order to accomplish my goals and dreams.

I grew up with my twin sister. When we were born, I weighed two pounds and my sister weighed four pounds. I had to remain in the hospital to gain weight and allow my organs to grow and mature. As a result, I developed a number of health challenges.

Challenge number one was that I had a severe allergy to dairy products. I actually had to drink Similac when I was nine years old, because it was the only dairy I could have. Once we jumped that hurdle, challenge number two arose. My hands and feet would frequently swell and the doctors could not figure out what was causing the issue. I was tested for all type of diseases like sickle cell, lupus and arthritis. Thankfully, as I grew up, I also somewhat grew out of those issues. At least they were not as prevalent as in my younger years.

During high school, I attended a vocational school for Certified Nursing Assistants. I did very well. I was nominated to be Vice President of our class for Health Occupational Students of America. I started working at nursing homes after school and every other weekend. I was extremely excited because I had graduated at the top of my class. I had planned to go to West Chester University's RN Program. I felt like I was on my way. My sister and I were scheduled to start school in the fall. A month before finalizing the paperwork for both of us to start school, challenge number three presented its ugly head. I got sick and had to have surgery.

This put a hole in my heart. Because of the money that my mom spent on my surgery, I could not start school until the next school year.

I was diagnosed with having a tumor the size of a basketball on my right ovary. The doctor informed my mom and me that I would be out of commission for a while.

Instantly, my young adult dreams were on hold.

After surgery, I was diagnosed with polycystic ovaries and endometriosis. I tried to figure out how this happened to me. The doctor asked my mom when I started my menses. When my mom told him that I was nine years old when it started, he explained that starting that young was the root cause of my issue. At that point, I was faced with a gigantic challenge—challenge number four. Now, what will Annie be? I'd always hoped that my carefully planned dreams would come to pass. Nonetheless, once my dream was derailed, the major challenge I battled was challenge number five. Speaking negatively became my way of life.

Fear began to control my thoughts and words. What if I can't have children? What if my husband wants children? Will I be able to bear children? Will he want to still be married to me with all of these female problems? All I began to ask myself was, *Who am I, now?*

Before a word is on
my tongue you know it
completely, O Lord.

Psalm 139:3

Who Am I?

Growth is often uncomfortable, messy, and full of feelings you weren't expecting, but it's necessary.

— Anonymous

All of the health challenges overwhelmed me, both physically and emotionally. I did not know what the next phase of my life would look like. We always try to do our best and look our best. We dress up, get our hair done and treat ourselves to manicures and pedicures to make us feel good on the outside, while on the inside, we are screaming, "DO YOU SEE ME?" We are asking, "Do you see the pain behind my smile?" "Do you sense that there is a wall of tears waiting to escape from my eyes?" "Does anyone see that I feel trapped in my body and that I feel alone, because I am convinced that no one understands what I am going through?"

I'd hear the scripture from Psalm 139 that tells me that, *I am fearfully and wonderfully made and marvelous in His eyes.*

Knowing that scripture did not make a difference for me then; fear had gripped my mind and caused me to doubt the word. My health challenges scarred me emotionally. I was not a size 10. I was a size 24 and all I ever heard was, she has a pretty face. The negative comments from others made me feel worthless, especially when I looked in the mirror.

FINDING ME
Reflections

*For we are his workmanship, created in Christ Je-
sus for good works, which God prepared before-
hand, that we should walk in them.*

— Ephesians 2:10

Take a moment and answer these questions:

1. When you look in the mirror, who do you see?

2. Describe what you see.

3. Were your words negative?

If your words were negative, let's start to change that
habit today. Pray this prayer with me.

Father, please forgive me for all the things I spoke over
myself during difficult situations and trials. Help me to see ME
the way you created me to be, as your daughter, beautifully
and wonderfully made and marvelous in your eyes. Amen.

Go back and look in the mirror again. Who do you see now?

I got married when I was twenty-two years old. I
weighed 167 pounds. I was happy with myself, for the most
part, but I still felt incomplete. My husband loved me and

would tell me how beautiful I was to him. I knew he meant it from his heart and I accepted his words. However, because my heart was shattered, I was unable to believe him.

My first surgery was at 18 years old. By the time I was 22 years old, I was on my third surgery due to issues with my reproductive system. I was diagnosed with endometriosis, which is a very scary disease because it blocks the fallopian tubes, and lines your uterus and pelvis. This disease put fear in my heart and I allowed this fear to make me think I might never be a mom. I also worried about how it would affect my intimacy with my spouse. Endometriosis can be very painful. It turns scar tissue into fibroids, which can cause major issues for a female's reproductive system. Here we go again, another health challenge had come to take my hopes and dreams away.

When I allowed fear to creep in, it was overwhelming. I felt like I was not whole or complete as a woman. I recall my mom saying that when my sister and I were born, the doctor informed her that one of us would not be able to conceive. I was beginning to feel like it would be me.

At the age of 35, I was told that I had to have a hysterectomy. My world came tumbling down. I was extremely upset and hurt. I remembered something else my mom said to me six months earlier. "Annie," my mom said, "Why keep something inside of you that's broke and can't be fixed?" I said, "Mom, John and I are believing and standing in faith

that God will perform a miracle. God did it for Sarah and Abraham. Surely, He can do it for us too." My mom replied, "God also gives us common sense too. Your body has been through so much." She was not faithless. She was concerned about me. At the time of our conversation, I was on my twelfth surgery.

The 12 Surgeries:

1—Polycystic Ovarian Cyst removed

7—Laser Laparoscopies for Endometriosis

3—Myomectomy (removal of fibroids)

1—Partial Hysterectomy

I was diagnosed with polycystic ovaries, endometriosis and fibroids. Polycystic ovaries is a hormonal disorder causing enlarged ovaries with small cysts on the outer edges. Fibroids are benign (not cancerous) tumors that spontaneously appear in the uterus. During my surgeries, I recall the doctor saying they removed two fibroids. One weighed three pounds and the other weighed four pounds. During another surgery, I had a fibroid that was so large that it spanned my uterus from the front to the back and had many smaller fibroids attached to it.

Having to endure so many surgeries was traumatic. Eventually, the doctors confirmed that I was infertile. John and I decided to try infertility treatments to see if that would enable us to become parents. We did six artificial insemination cycles but none of them worked. We did three IVF cycles and we had three embryos transferred. We were praying that this would be the answer to us becoming parents. After we had the embryos transferred, we got the news that one embryo had attached itself to the uterus. We began to pray, "Lord let this work." I was at work and I got the call from the nurse. "Mrs. Murray," she asked, "Yes," I nervously answered. "CONGRATULA-TIONS! You're pregnant." I could not stop crying. I called my hubby and told him, "Honey, WE'RE PREGNANT!" We were both filled with joy.

The nurse said you have to come in tomorrow to get blood work again. I was so excited that the procedure worked. I went to get my blood work done to make sure that my FSH (follicle-stimulating hormone) level was going up. I went back to work and was so full of joy. My phone rang again. It was a different nurse this time. I answered and she said, "Annette, you're not pregnant." I was confused. I asked, "What happened? A nurse just called and told me that I was pregnant. She gave me my FSH level." "I'm so sorry," she told me, "She shouldn't't have called you, until we did blood work today." I was distraught.

We did everything we were supposed to do for this to work and in the process, we exhausted all of our savings. We tried to control having children, by doing it on our own. However, my having children wasn't a part of God's plan. My heart was crushed and I could not understand why all of this was happening. That day I told my husband, "John, I do not want to hurt you. I will release you to go marry someone else." I knew we both wanted a family, and it was evident that I could not have children. We cried and held one another. My husband said, "Look at me Honey, IF WE NEVER HAVE ANY CHILDREN TOGETHER, AS LONG AS WE'RE TOGETHER, THAT'S ALL THAT MATTERS." That glorious and harmonious act of love was straight from his heart.

Before long, FEAR came and tried to grip me. "You can't have children. You aren't a woman." These horrible thoughts played over and over in my head. I began to beat myself over it. I also became deeply depressed.

I could not celebrate with anyone who was having a baby. I could not go to baby showers. It hurt me to see someone else pregnant and happy.

I felt alone and was convinced that no one really understood my pain. Rejection, fear, anxiety and depression were all hiding beneath my pain. I would only eat one meal a day, but they were the wrong foods. I gained so much weight, that I totally lost sight of who I was and who I belonged to. Food became my source. One day I looked at myself and only saw a person who I could not recognize. I weighed 336 pounds

FINDING ME
Reflections

I will look unto the hills from whence cometh my help.

— Psalms 121:1

1. What things do you resort to, when faced with opposition?

2. Does it bring satisfaction to your life?

3. Have you overcome the opposition?

Let us fix our eyes on Jesus the author and finisher of our faith.

Hebrews 12:2

The Pain and Agony

*In the pain, the agony, and the heroic endeavors of
life, we pass through a refiner's fire, and the insig-
nificant and the unimportant in our lives can melt
away like dross and make our faith bright, intact
and strong.*

— James E. Faust

When you think about all the things that you have been
through, sometimes you cannot fathom how you made it
through every time. My pain and scars were so deep that,
eventually, I could not imagine what things would look like
without them. The scars were constant reminders of what
I had to go through every day, month, and year. I became
great at wearing a mask and making sure that I looked the
part, but inside I was CRUSHED!

After I had the partial hysterectomy and after my mom
passed away, I never dealt with the pain, suffering or grief
that I was experiencing. Five months prior to my hyster-

ectomy, John and I were asked to take on a role in our lives that *was* part of my dream. It was evident now, that becoming parents was presented to us in a different way. We had the opportunity to care for an amazing, beautiful baby girl. Parenting her brought joy to our lives. However, something was still not quite right. There were times when my husband would say, "Honey, you love her, but something is wrong." I told him I was afraid to become attached in case the adoption did not go through. I recall how my friends and co-workers wanted this so much for us, that they paid for all of the lawyer and court fees. We were ecstatic and amazed at how God's love was shown to us. We followed the adoption process closely and moved into our new place. Social services visited and made sure that our home was safe. I called the attorney's office to let them know that we received our background checks and the other documents that were needed. My life then faced another heartbreaking challenge. The lawyer informed us that the birth mom had withdrawn from the adoption process. We were given twenty-four hours and then we had to give the baby back.

I WAS DEVASTATED, SHOCKED, CONFUSED, HURT and COMPLETELY NUMB!

The shock that I experienced was so severe, that I was taken to the emergency room. The doctors thought I had a suffered a stroke. The entire left side of my body was drooping.

I had a complete nervous breakdown.

The way my husband cared for me was amazing. He was attentive, considerate and sensitive to the mental, emotional and physical impact that having to give our baby back had on me. I was out of work for five months.

One of the worst parts about all of this is that I worked in maternity case management. I eventually could not continue working in the same position. Having to speak with other pregnant women, in light of what I was going through, was just too hard for me.

All this happened in 2003. My mom passed that February and we got the baby at four weeks old in May. I had a partial hysterectomy in October. I never grieved my mom's passing.

There are no words to describe what I felt at that time. I went to counseling and I could not make it through the sessions. It was entirely too much. My boss found me another position working for her BRCA Genetic Testing. I was the first non-clinical staff to complete the program. I won so many awards and I felt incredibly good, because my mind and thoughts were pre-occupied with studying, instead of with the other things that were going on in my life. All of this happened in a nine- month period of time.

As I was recovering from the nervous breakdown, the little girl we almost adopted got sick. Her parents called to let us know she was in the hospital. They allowed us to see her. The look on her face when she saw us, was happy and sad. Her facial expressions said, "Where have you been?" "Why did you leave me?". It was so good to see her, but it also brought back the pain of having to let her go.

FINDING ME
Reflections

I will look unto the hills from whence cometh my help.

— Psalms 121:1

1. Have you gone through a traumatic situation that you erased from your mind but never really healed from?

2. When you reminisce, does the pain resurface?

3. How did you address and resolve the pain?

The baby got better and her mom realized that she remembered John and me. She wanted us to have time with the baby, so she brought the baby to see us. During my time of my recovery, the Lord ministered to me. He wanted me to learn how to love unconditionally. When I realized this, I initially thought to myself, "Lord what about me? I have suffered so much. Why do I have to be the one to love unconditionally." Although the process was awfully hard for me to manage, the Lord kept teaching me. He was patient with me. One day the baby's mom allowed us to visit and her mom and I had some alone time. The baby's mother said, "I don't know what to say, but I want to apologize for what I put you through. Can you forgive me?" My mind raced through all the things I wanted to say. I wanted to tell her how hurt I was. I wanted to ask her why she couldn't just be honest with us, so that we would not have had to go down this road. Those were the questions in my mind. Nevertheless, the Holy Spirit had already been dealing with my heart. He had been healing the deep hurt.

With tears rolling down my face, I told her that God taught me how to love unconditionally and that because He has forgiven me, that I must forgive her. We were both emotional wrecks at that moment. I will never forget the pain and agony of that phase of my life, but because of the Grace of God, I live a FREE LIFE knowing that God's love covered me!

FINDING ME
Reflections

I will look unto the hills from whence cometh my help.

— Psalms 121:1

1. What are you attached to?

2. What do you feel is the root cause of you attaching yourself to this thing?

3. Who do you need to forgive and receive freedom for your life?

Fear not, for I have redeemed you. I have called you by name, you are mine.

Isaiah 43:1

But one thing I do, forgetting those things which are behind and reaching forward to those things which are ahead. I press toward the goal for the prize of the upward call of God in Christ Jesus.

Philippians 3:12

The thief comes to steal and kill and destroy. I came that they may have life and have it abundantly.

John 10:10

If we confess our sins, he is faithful and will forgive us our sins and purify us from all unrighteousness.

1 John 1:9

Set Back for a Set Up

Every setback means you're one step closer to seeing the dream come to pass.

— Joel Osteen

After having the twelfth surgery in 2003, I was finally able to close the door on having surgeries. At that point, it was also totally and completely clear that I could not have children. After the little girl was taken back by her mother, I figured I would just close the door to that chapter of my life and keep moving forward. I did not know what living without the hope of being a mother would be like, but I was determined to press my way forward. Over the next several years, I became incredibly involved in my job with helping to open new offices and training new staff. As a matter of fact, in 2005, I was promoted to management. I threw myself into my work and focused on helping my staff to achieve their goals. I was active in church, helped with programming, sang with my husband's group, taught a Bible Isaiah class and tried to be a good wife to my husband.

How many of you know that you cannot have a healthy relationship in marriage by being so busy, that you don't take the time to take care of your first priority? I was doing the work of the Lord, but I was not really taking care of the main thing—my husband and my relationship. Being busy helped to ease the pain of all of the loss. However, it was not a healthy way of dealing with things. One day, my husband was driving to work and said, "Babe we are on the move too much and we don't spend quality time together." We both agreed that a change was necessary.

Around the same time that John and I agreed to make the adjustments that we needed to make in order to spend more quality time with one another, my job made me a Subject Matter Expert (SME) for a new system they'd acquired for clinical staff. Once the Pennsylvania staff was trained, I was scheduled to travel to Houston every other week from May 2007 to October 2007 to get the office up and running. I was very excited because I love to travel and help people. One Monday morning, my husband was driving to work and the Lord gave him these words:

I shall have what I decree
Yes, I believe it belongs to me
So, I am going to speak into the atmosphere

He began to sing the words and explained to me how strongly the song spoke to his spirit. At that time, John was also very busy. He was traveling to play guitar for his group and other artists, helping at the church, writing music and producing songs. Later that afternoon, he was sitting at his desk at work and his friend, who he used to play with at a church in Philly, called him. His friend had landed a job as Executive Director of Music at a mega-church, so he'd recently moved to Texas. "What are you doing?" he asked my husband. John replied, "Wishing I was doing what you are doing." The friend said, "Well, that's what I'm calling you for. I want to know if you will come to Dallas and interview for our church's Director of Praise and Worship opening. We were so excited and amazed at how John had just written that song. God had heard his cry! You will have what you decree. Declare and decree the promises of God over your life.

Interestingly, I was scheduled to travel to Houston on the same weekend that the church had requested that John come to interview. Earlier that year, my pastor said to me, "You're going to move to Texas." "I don't think so," I replied.

The weekend arrived and it was time for John and me to travel to Dallas. We had an incredible experience. We were grateful for the opportunity to visit the mega-church. After a couple of weeks, my husband got a call to come back for another interview. We went back for the second interview. When he arrived, they said, "We wanted you to come back, so we could tell you in person that we want to hire you." John was ecstatic. I was simultaneously ecstatic and scared because now, we *were* moving to Texas. I have always lived in Pennsylvania near my family. What our Pastor prophesied, came to pass. My husband would start his new position by Thanksgiving, which was two weeks away. Talk about a life-changing experience taking place right before our eyes. The move was quick and I was afraid because this would be our first time living in two different locations. I cried. This was a big move and we had no family and friends in Dallas.

FINDING ME
Reflections

Before they call, I will answer; while they are still speaking, I will hear.

— Isaiah 65:24

But Jesus replied, "My Father is always working, and so am I."

— John 5:17

1. Have you ever been a situation in which you experienced a spontaneous move of God?

2. How did you feel?

Sometimes God has to do a quick work because He knows that we are stubborn. As my husband transitioned to move and live in Texas, my heart was in a state of panic. I was anxious. At that time, my job was still based in Pennsylvania. The cost of living is different in Pennsylvania than it is in Texas. My boss asked me one day, "Why aren't you excited for this great new journey?" I replied, "I still don't have a job!" She matter-of-factly said, "Annette, why don't you work from home?" I was shocked and pleasantly surprised!

"You would allow me to work from home?" I asked. She replied, "Yes! I would not want to lose you as one of my management team members. Let's follow the policies and procedures. Speak with your immediate boss. When she comes to me, I'll let her know that I'm in agreement." I spoke with my manager and she agreed that I could work from home. However, I needed to wait until March 2008. I was disappointed about how long I had to wait but was still very grateful that working from home was an option for me. I moved in with my sister and her husband, while my hubby was living in temporary housing, until we could find a permanent home. I thanked God for the favor, but I did not want to live apart from my husband that long. One Sunday morning, one of the Associate Pastors told John that she had the perfect house for him. She said that she could meet with him the next day. The next day John went to see the duplex, which was perfect for us. God blessed us so much, that it was almost unbelievable. The Pastor and the others from the church surprised him and had living room furniture, a refrigerator and a bed for him. He was happy and I was even more excited because he was able to quickly get settled into our new home. My friends and I drove to Texas from Pennsylvania. I packed the house up and the storage company picked up the storage cube to be delivered near Christmas. It took us 26 hours to drive. We praised God for his hand of protection through rain, sleet and snow. I kept calling my husband, saying, "I'm so exhausted. I have so much to do once I get there. I wanted to take care of my friends who helped drive our cars to Texas." Like the amazing husband he is, John kept telling me, "Honey, it's going to be fine. Just get here, so I can see you!" Despite my mind racing about how much we had to do, he kept reassuring me that all would be well.

When we arrived at the house, it was so cute. It was just right for my husband and me. He said, "Honey, look how God met our needs. A family took me to the market today. Look, the freezer and refrigerator are FULL." The cabinets as well as the pantry was full. TEARS, TEARS, TEARS! All I needed to do was rest and spend time with my husband.

God is faithful! Just believe that ALL THINGS are POSSIBLE through Him.

FINDING ME
Reflections

For we walk by faith, not by sight.

— II Corinthians 5:7

1. Are there things that you keep worrying about in your life?

2. Why does it take so much to trust God and take Him at his word?

My God shall supply all of
your needs according to his
riches in glory
by Christ Jesus.

Philippians 4:19

The New Beginning

Take the first step in faith. You don't have to see the whole staircase, just take the first step.
— Martin Luther King Jr.

When I returned to Pennsylvania, I worked every day and deeply missed my hubby. So that we could spend Christmas and the New Year together, I made plans to go see him over the holiday break. One day, while I was working, my boss looked at me and said, "You can go home!" It was a slow day and most of the offices were closed. I said, "No, my sister and family are still at work. I'll be there by myself." She said, "GO HOME!" I said, "No, I don't want to." I still didn't get it! She said it so that I understood exactly what she meant this time, "Annette, you can move to Texas. Your work-at-home set up is complete." Stunned, I asked, "I don't have to wait until March?" "No," she said, "This is your Christmas gift!" Tears began to run down my face. I was so excited. I could not wait to call John and tell him that I was able to come to our new home in Texas. I could finally be with my hubby, so that we could start our new journey together.

I started working from home and loved it. Except for the occasional technical issues, I felt like I was still in Pennsylvania. I started to feel happier because things were turning around for John and me. We were full of joy and our lives had taken on such a celebratory mood.

The home we were staying in, was a temporary housing situation. However, we eventually found a home that we could lease, until we became more familiar with the Dallas area. We packed everything up and moved a few miles down the road to our new home, which was bigger than the previous house. I was upstairs about to get dressed. I suddenly felt kind of weak. As I began to call my husband, I felt myself going down. I fainted.

We called my doctor in Pennsylvania. I had my twelfth surgery in 2003 and we thought that everything was fine now. We were sure that there would not be any more surgeries. My doctor said that he did not want to take the risk of me flying back home. He said that flying in the state I was in, could be detrimental to my health. He asked that we give him a couple of hours, so that he could contact an associate in one of the Dallas hospitals. When he called back, the doctor told us to go the St. Paul's emergency room. One of his associates could examine me to make sure that I was okay. The hospital was about 45 minutes away from our new home.

We had no clue where the hospital was located. A friend came over to take us there. When we got there, they were waiting for me to arrive. They took us to the back and said that they were going to take x-rays. As the tech was taking the x-ray, I heard him say loudly and clearly, "Oh my goodness. This is not good!"

Immediately, fear gripped me. Anyone could see from my facial expression, that I was terrified. That is when the tech realized that I had heard what she said to herself. She tried to reassure me that all was well, but I didn't believe her.

When I arrived back at the room, I said, "Honey, I heard the tech say, 'Oh my goodness. This is not good!" John calmly replied, "We shall believe the report of the Lord." My hubby kept encouraging me to have faith. He never stopped telling me that everything was going to be alright. My entire body was shaking from fear and from being nervous. About ten minutes later, a doctor came into the room and asked, "Why were you seeing an OB Oncologist in Pennsylvania?" I replied, "Because I had polycystic ovaries, fibroids and endometriosis." She proceeded to tell me that I had a 14-centimeter mass attached to all of my organs and that it was cancer. EVERYTHING in my body went completely NUMB. She then instructed me that I needed to see the OB Oncologist right away. She explained that she had we scheduled an appointment for me to see the doctor at 10:00 am that Friday.

Once again, we felt like our world was CRUSHED!

Lord,

"Lord, I thought all of this was done and that I was on the road to recovery!" I called my twin sister and my two aunts. We were all like, "Jesus what's happening?" On Friday morning, my hubby and I went to the oncologist's office. It was the scariest thing I have ever experienced. Seeing all the patients that were there dealing with their cancer battles was overwhelming. While we were waiting, I began to pray for them and forget about myself. They called us back to be seen by the doctor. After about ten minutes, she arrived to tell us what the x-ray and MRI reports showed.

She said that I had to have extensive surgery and that it would be a long process to get through. She explained that I would need to have one procedure to remove the mass and that I would be in ICU for a couple of days post-surgery. After that, I would go through another surgery to check my lymph nodes and to make sure the cancer had not spread. She also informed us that there was a strong possibility of me having a colostomy bag. Tears ran down both of our faces. John and I were so overwhelmed with this information, that we thought we were in the world by ourselves at that moment. I said to the doctor "Okay, let me check with my boss to request the time off. "We can probably schedule the surgery in a couple of weeks." The doctor said, "Oh, no. Your surgery is scheduled for Tuesday." "This Tuesday—in four days?" I asked. "Yes!" she said. Fear completely overtook me and I started to cry.

FINDING ME
Reflections

1. What life experienced have you encountered that completely took your mind captive?

While I was going through pre-admission testing. John called my sister and other family members. We both were baffled! We had just moved to Texas five months earlier and had just moved into our new home over the weekend. Hundreds of questions and negative thoughts ran through my mind. What did I do wrong? Why is this happening to me? Will I die? Can my family get here in time for me to have the surgery? My sister, aunts, and pastor came, as soon as they could get a flight to Texas.

My friends planned a surprise pre-fortieth birthday celebration. All of this happened in April. My birthday was in May, so they figured, "Let's celebrate now." As the doctor had advised, she was not sure how long I would be down. It was an extremely sweet gesture and they made me feel loved. I was bursting with tears, because I wished my mom were still alive to be with me. My mom and both of my grandmothers had never missed any of my surgeries.

I did not feel well at all, but we went to church that Sunday morning. I wanted to make it to church, because I was not sure when I would make it back again. As service started, my husband shared with the congregation that his wife received an ugly report from the doctor and made sure to add that we would believe the report of the Lord. He began to sing *To Worship You I Live.* That was my first time hearing the song. I cried and prayed and prayed and cried. After the service, I told John that I did not feel well and that I could I have a fever. I could barely walk out of the sanctuary.

As we headed toward the parking lot, through an exit door that Bishop and First Lady used, First Lady saw me and said, "Mrs. Murray, I've been waiting to meet you." I could barely stand from being so weak. She embraced me and I felt strength come into my body, as she called on the Name of Jesus. She did not even know my entire situation. After her embrace, I was able to exit the building and get to the car. That night I was trying to prepare my work for my co-supervisors to take over, while I was out. It was extremely challenging for me. I could not stop crying. I just wanted to know why I was I going through this again. Another surgery? This was surgery thirteen.

My pastor, Brenda Cuthbertson, Aunt Maxine, Aunt Marie and my sister, Tracey, prepared everything for Tuesday morning. They made sure my home was clean and that everything would be easy for John, while I was hospitalized. Pastor Cuthbertson said, "I put blessed oil on my hands, so that I can anoint every doctor and nurse who enters your room." My doctor's assistant came in and drew on my stomach. The fear came back again even stronger than the day I heard the nurse say. "Omg, this is not good." The pastor and my aunts began to pray to calm my nerves. My doctor walked into the room and she said, "Mr. Murray, I have a question for you?" He said, "Yes, Ma'am." "Was that you who was singing at church on Sunday?" she asked.

I will never forget the surprised look on all of our faces! "Doctor," I said, "You go to the Megachurch?" "Yes, she answered. "Mrs. Murray, when you two left my office on Friday, I was so concerned. I did not how I was going to do your surgery," she said. "This is so complicated," the doctor told us she said to God. "But, Mr. Murray, when you sang that song, *To Worship You I Live* for your wife and then Bishop preached, the Lord started to show me during the message, the map of how to do your surgery."

I had to stop writing my story just now, to give God praise! Hallelujah, Glory to God, Thank you Jesus! God You are amazing and You are faithful.

Yes! My doctor, hubby and I were all at the same service praying about the same surgery—my surgery.

Where two or three are gathered together in my name, there I am in the midst.

— Matthew 18:20

We all began to rejoice because we knew without a doubt that God was in control. I said, "Thank you Jesus! My doctor knows you *and* she was in church with us *and she is also* trusting you to take care of things." The doctor said it would not be easy and let us know that the surgery would take three to four hours. However, she was allowing up to seven hours for my surgery. I immediately asked my husband to please sing before they took me back. I began to cry and worship God. I kept singing even after they had put the oxygen mask on my face to start the anesthesia before the operation.

When I came out of recovery, I was admitted into a Presidential Suite in a private area of the hospital. I was not sure how I was able to get that hospital room. I was surprised. The nurses were asking, "Who is she that she's in this room?" I thank God for the favor that was extended to me. I was in so much pain. When my family shared what the doctor had told them, I learned that the doctor was able to remove the tumor and that it was huge. They also told me that we had to wait a couple of days for the pathology report.

My first night was pretty rough. My stomach had been cut both vertically and horizontally. The next day, a nurse with red hair came in to give me a breathing treatment. "Mmmm," she hummed. "I feel the glory of the Lord in this room." I looked at her and said, "Okay, praise God." She said it again,"I feel the glory of the Lord in this room." She started clapping her hands and jumping all around the room repeating she felt the glory of the Lord in the room. She went into the bathroom and repeated it again. I just prayed in the spirit and said, "Okay Lord, whatever you're doing right now in this room, I receive it." The entire time the breathing machine she was supposed to use to administer my treatment, was still just sitting on the tray. She came out of the bathroom and left the room. I chuckled and said, "Thank you Lord for my treatment today." The whole scene was very funny and heartwarming. What an experience!

FINDING ME
Reflections

The Lord your God is in your midst, a mighty one who will save; he will rejoice over you with gladness; he will quiet you by. His love; he will exult over you with loud singing.

— Zephaniah 3:17

1. Has anything like this ever happened to you? Has anyone ever started praising and worshipping God to change the atmosphere where you were?

The next day the doctor came in and told her assistant, "I will be in here with Mrs. Murray for about an hour. Please do not disturb us." I had a scared look on my face, as if to say, "Uh oh! What now?" She said, "Annie, I wanted to tell you that the day that you and John came to see me was my last day at the Cancer Clinic. My husband and children moved to another state. They're waiting for me to come be there with them." She continued, "I knew when you were in my office, that there was something special about you. However, I didn't know what it was, until Sunday, when we were all at church. Your situation was pretty challenging, so I'm going to postpone leaving until we get you better." Tears fell down my face, as

I thanked God for favor with Him and with my doctor. She told me that she had placed a drain in my abdomen because of the fluid they had to put inside of me, so that they could remove the tumor. She emphatically told me, "YOU CANNOT HAVE ANY MORE ABDOMINAL SURGERIES, UNLESS IT IS LIFE OR DEATH"! "Oh, no. What's wrong?" I asked her. She explained that because of all of the surgeries I had, my organs are meshed together. For example, she said, "We can't remove your cervix without splitting your bladder in half. If you have another abdominal surgery, there is a mortality rate of 99%." I was in shock once again, and I was glad to be alive. The pathology report showed that the tumor the doctors removed was benign. I had a rough road of recovery ahead, but I was willing to fight my way back to health. My family members flew into Texas every other week to assist John with caring for me. My recovery was very hard. I had thrush in my mouth and I couldn't eat because of all the antibiotics. My drain had to be changed three times a day. However, through every second of it, my incredible husband never flinched. He never got upset when he had to change my drain. He unpacked it and then repacked it with new gauze. I experienced true love. John made the vows we took on our wedding day come alive. He loved and cared for me "in sickness and in health." He went to work, came home and took care of me. My family and friends helped out by cooking meals for us. It was a terribly hard process to get through, but together we did.

FINDING ME
Reflections

*Brothers and sisters, I do not consider myself yet to
have taken hold of it. But one thing I do: Forgetting
what is behind and straining toward what is ahead,
I press on toward the goal to win the prize for which
God has called me heavenward in Christ Jesus.*

— Philippians 3:13-14

1. Have you kept pressing your way through a challenging or life-changing situation?

2. What were some of the things you did to keep going?

My pressing on power came through my times of
prayer and worship, by speaking in faith that God was going to bring me through. I tried to remain positive and let
my body heal.

Once, I wound up having an infection in the drain
and was readmitted to the hospital. As I laid in the hospital bed, I kept saying, "I can't give up. God please give me
the strength to keep going." It was hard to believe that my
healing was going to ever take place, because one day all
was well and the next day something else would go wrong.
However, by the grace of God, I made it through.

Reality

It is difficult to say what is impossible, for the dream of yesterday is the hope of today and the reality of tomorrow.

— Robert H. Goddard

I had made it through so much, that I had become numb and out of sorts. I let everything go. I did not care how much I ate or what I looked like. I never looked at myself in the mirror. I would buy clothes and act as if I weren't getting bigger. I was wearing a size 26-28. Anyone who was paying attention could tell that I didn't love myself. I loved to make myself look pretty, carry cute purses and wear nice dresses and shoes, but inside I was CRUSHED from all that I had been through in life.

I had a blessed marriage, good job, a nice home and a nice car. However, we know it is not the material things that make us love ourselves. I would do everything for everyone, except me. As a matter of fact, I would do whatever anyone asked of me without hesitation. I wanted to make other people happy, but I was suffering silently inside. Eventually, I started to realize how much I didn't love myself. I would start projects and stop them because I could not stand to be alone. I enjoyed being creative with making party favors, event planning and serving others. I always had to be doing something with others to feel like I was someone.

Since I was not able to have children, I felt like people sometimes did not include me because I wasn't a mom. I worked on my job for nineteen years and I loved what I did, until my job was job eliminated. When I lost my job, I felt like I totally lost myself. I just didn't know who I was anymore. I didn't have a job. I didn't have the same friends as I did when I was at home in Pennsylvania. What was I supposed to do now?

Around the time that I was pondering all of these questions and trying to find myself, my husband met a guy from Brazil and they became good friends. He asked my husband to do a worship conference in Brazil called Uma So Voz (Only One Voice). His family came to Texas to meet John, take photos and do promotional videos in preparation for him to come to their country. The gentleman's father spoke and his son interpreted from Portuguese to English for us. The man told John to tell him that they did not believe in a husband coming to Brazil alone, if he had a wife. They told us that they wanted me to come with my husband to do ministry with him. I didn't know what type of ministry they were expecting. However, the Pastor asked if I would preach one night of the conference. We prayed and I said, "Yes, I will speak at the conference."

This was the beginning of my life being changed for the good—forever.

We traveled to Brazil in 2013. It was a life changing experience. God showed me the greatest love.

After preaching and praying for people, all of their children began to come swarm around and hug me. The children were calling me their American mommy. Tears of joy filled my eyes and my heart was overwhelmed with my heavenly Father's love and with the children's love for me.

FINDING ME
Reflections

See what great love the Father has lavished on us, that we should be called children of God! And that is what we are!

— 1 John 3:1

1. Have you ever had something happen to you, to remind you of the Father's extravagant love for you?

When we returned from Brazil, many children started to come into my life. I already have several nieces, nephews and godchildren. There is also a special person, who is actually my relative but is more like a daughter to me. However, even with having all of these wonderful people in my life, it still felt like there was a void.

I'd never earned a college degree, so that was another regret hidden beneath my pain. I was working in different places and felt like I was not accepted. It was because, from their perspective, I didn't look like them or I didn't have what they thought I should have. I wasn't accepted as a female preacher, because where we attended church, women were not acknowledged as ministers at that time. I felt unwanted. When I would travel and people would make fun of my size, I'd feel crushed again. The words that would come out of my mouth were, "I'm so FAT. Yes, I am a big girl. I didn't know how to describe myself, without using those words. I would pray but I wouldn't listen to what God was saying to me. Something started to click in my mind. "It's not them. It's YOU! You're doing this to yourself." That was the truth. The truth began to settle in more, as my health started failing me in other areas.

FINDING ME
Reflections

Life and death are in the power of the tongue.
— Proverbs 18:21

1. Are you aware of the words you used to describe yourself?

I could speak encouraging words to everyone but myself. I didn't realize that I was slowing killing myself in every way.

My mind and body were not healthy. I was an emotional basket case. I began to read the word of God, but I didn't know how to apply it, because I was in denial.

I had to get my mind back in the right place, in order to begin healing. I began to study what the Bible says about how I need to use my words. I had to start there, but it also had to start with my heart. For many years, I had spoken negatively about what my heart felt from all of the pain, challenges and ups and downs. I had allowed that negativity to fester.

For out of the abundance of the heart the mouth speaks.
— Matthew 12:34

I began to cry and ask the Father to forgive me for the years of speaking negativity to and about myself. I prayed, like King David, that God would deliver and heal my heart. I asked him to renew a right spirit within me. I pleaded with Him to purge me with His hyssop and make me whiter than snow.

The mouth of the righteous
is a fountain of life, but
the mouth of the wicked
conceals violence.

Proverbs 10:11

Facing The Fear

You gain strength, courage and confidence by every experience in which you really stop to look fear in the face. You are able to say to yourself, 'I have lived through this horror. I can take the next thing that comes along.' You must do the thing you think you cannot do.

— Eleanor Roosevelt

The more that I sought God, the more the Holy Spirit spoke to my spirit. He gave me insight about the crushings that I'd gone through. He explained that the trials I endured were similar to the crushing process that an olive goes through, in order to provide us with its precious oil.

I researched and learned that the variety and maturation of the olives influences the quality and taste of the oil that it produces. Wow! I'd certainly survived a variety of situations that had matured me. As I continued to read, it explained that olives used to be hand-picked but that now they are harvested. In the harvesting process, a variety of shakers transmit vibrations through the tree branches causing the olives to drop into nets that are placed underneath the tree. After harvesting, the olives that have fallen from the tree are washed to remove the dirt, leaves and twigs. The olive is then ready to be processed into oil.

Through my studies, I began to see how God had taken me through a shaking and cleansing process so that—like the oil extracted from the olive—He could extract from me an anointing that would be used to benefit others. Hallelujah, thank you Jesus! All along, God had a plan for me.

> *For I know the plans I have for you, declares the Lord, plans to prosper you and not to harm you, plans to give you hope and a future.*
> — Jeremiah 29:11

If you recall earlier in the book, I'd mentioned that I could not look at myself in the mirror. One day, the Holy Spirit told me to look at myself. Hesitantly, I turned to look at myself sideways in the mirror. The Holy Spirit said again, "Look at your entire body. Look at yourself." Tears began to fall down my face. I heard the Father say to me, "You are my daughter and you are loved!" I could not stop crying.

Then questions began to come to mind.

Who are you? I mumbled, "I am a daughter of God."

Who are you? I mumbled, "I am a daughter of God."

Who are you? I mumbled, "I am a daughter of God."

After I said it the third time, something began to come alive inside of me. I started to believe what I heard myself say. I began to say it again and again, each time with more power and authority.

Who do you see? "I see His beloved and cherished daughter."

Who do you see? " I see a beautiful vessel."

Who are you? "I am a daughter of the Most High King."

The tears just kept flowing down my face. The spirit of the Lord was upon me right there in my home. He was filling up my cup. I kept speaking life to myself. I am beautiful. I am fearfully and wonderfully made. I am a conqueror. I am a winner. I have the victory. I am HEALED. I am DELIVERED. I am SET FREE and I am LOVED!

That day changed my life. I came ALIVE again. I am redeemed by the blood of the lamb and so are you.

FINDING ME
Reflections

Stop what you are doing right now and start speaking the positive words of God over yourself. SPEAK LIFE INTO THE ATMOSPHERE NOW.

> *Gentle words bring life and health.*
> — Proverbs 15:4

> *Kind words are like honey. Sweet to the soul and health for the body.*
> — Proverbs 16:24

> *A person's words can be life giving water; words of true wisdom are refreshing as a bubbling brook.*
> — Proverbs 18:3

As the years passed, I realized how much God loved me and how he demonstrated that love to me by extending my life. I fought through much trauma, hurt and pain but God allowed me to live and not die. I am so thankful that, by the Grace of God, my Spirit was also revived.

I always enjoyed helping others and making them happy. However, I could never clearly articulate what really made me happy. Isn't that something? I could talk about everything else but I did not know how to talk about what made me happy. I am grateful for everything that God has done in my life. True joy does not come from having things. It comes from being connected to the Father. For some apparent reason, when it came down to my life, I was scared about being happy about something special in my life. It seemed like every time I would get happy; something would snuff the joy out of me. You hear people quote the scripture that says the joy of the Lord is their strength. However, I couldn't feel joy, until we went back to Brazil. There, with all of my children, God began to show me what joy and strength looked like for me.

I was slowly healing. I was becoming who God created me to be. Some days were tougher than others, but all in all I felt God awakening my Spirit. He was restoring me and my story of pain and agony was being turned into a story of victory. God's glory was continuing to be revealed in my life.

For I reckon that the suffering of this present time, are not worthy to be compared with the glory which shall be revealed in us.

— Romans 8:18

God blessed me with two spiritual Mothers, who walked with me through my hurt and pain. They took time to teach me and talk to me about the sensitive things in my life. When they would say certain phrases, I felt like my mom was talking through them to me. They helped me to see that the pain in my life had caused me to be emotional and sensitive. I finally learned how to channel those feelings, so I could receive what God was trying to do in me and through me for others. God was maturing. Sometimes it hurt and sometimes I felt immediate joy.

The Holy Spirit continued to speak and reveal where God wanted me to be and who He called me to be. The Father's love gave me what my heart longed for—

I was born to live, love and believe in who I am! I stopped caring what others thought about what I should do or where I should go. The Holy Spirit said I have already given you authority. Activate your authority and walk in it! I have validated you daughter. All I could see was my will, instead of asking God what His will was for my life. Finally, I'd learn to say what really mattered to God, "Thine will be done, Father."

FINDING ME
Reflections

1. Are you looking for affirmation from someone or something?

2. Do you know that God has given you authority?

3. Can you see what God sees for your life?

I must admit there have been things I once held onto. Sin was to blame. It was my own fault for causing you pain. I've been awakened to stir the flame. Burn it up, burn it, here in your presence, we lift it up.

— Stirring the Flame
by John Murray

All I could hear was wake up! Wake up!! Wake up!! Your plans are distorted! You have a bad view! I could hear God asking me, "Can't you see My hand on your life?" "Can't you see where I have brought you from?" Just like the harvesters shake the olive tree to loosen the olives and cause them to fall off of the branches, I have shaken your life up, to get the absolute best out of you. God's voice was loud and clear. He settled me even more, when I heard Him say, "Your thoughts are not my thoughts. Your ways are not my ways! Daughter, the path you are on is my perfect and absolute will."

> *The secret things belong to the Lord our God, but the things that are revealed belong to us and to our children forever, that we may do all the words of his law.*
>
> — Deuteronomy 29:29

> *I cry out to God, most High, to God who fulfills his purpose for me.*
>
> — Psalm 57:2

I had to understand God's purpose for my life, so I could live my abundant life.

God's sovereign will is His supreme authority and all things are under His control. When I took my focus off of what I wanted and put my focus on the things of God, my purpose began to speak loud and clear. My heart became lighter, my eyes began to open and my ears started to hear the Holy Spirit.

What happened, Annie?

I STARTED TO BELIEVE IN MYSELF! YES, I BEGAN TO BELIEVE!

When I took my mind off of things that were negative, I became more aware of who I was called to be. The lyrics to this song are what helped me.

Give thanks in all
circumstances for this is
God's will for you in Christ
Jesus.

1 Thessalonians 5:18

FINDING ME
Reflections

For it is God's will that by doing good, you should silence the ignorant talk of foolish people.

— I Peter 2:15

1. WHO ARE YOU LISTENING TO? Is it helping you? Is it keeping you from doing what you desire to do?

Pray with me: *Father, I RELEASE every negative person in my life that keeps me in a bad mood, negative, and disgruntled. Show me how to pray for or help them to be released from their life of negativity. In Jesus' Name. Amen.*

Keep Believing

*I believe that God you are my healer. I believe
you'll make me whole again. I believe you raised
me by your power. Lord, I believe everything you
promised I believe.*

— Jamar Jones

Everything may not be perfect. Everything may not be exactly like you want it to be. However, I am very thankful because I know God is going to bring you through. I'm so thankful for where He's brought me. I am so grateful that now, I am FREE to be ME!

To God be the Glory. Let go and let God do the work in you, so that you can live believing in YOURSELF! You can do all things through Christ, who strengthens you.

God promised He would always be with us. Even when it gets a little challenging, keep believing! When you feel like no one understands, keep believing. We often look for the big things, but God is in the small things too. Do not count those small steps out. They mean something in your process. Greater is coming in your life. Believe in the God in you, so that you can believe in YOURSELF!

Whatever it takes to keep yourself going, take those steps one at a time and don't stop. God said, He'll go before you. Believe His will and plan for your life. I speak life to you today and say, "GO FORTH!" Yes, you can do it!

Remember God has not
given you the spirit of fear,
but of power, love, and a
sound mind.

2 Timothy 1:7

You need to persevere, so that when you have done the will of God, you will receive what He promised.

Hebrews 10:36

I Believed I Could, So I did!

That's my story!

About the Author

Annette Trina Murray was born in Abington, Pennsylvania to the late Jacqueline Wiley and Larry Wiley. Annette has a twin sister, Antoinette Tracey Harris. Annette grew up in North Hills, Pennsylvania where she attended schools in the Upper Dublin School District. While attending high school, Annette also  attended Eastern Montgomery County Vocational Technical School to become a Certified Nursing Assistant. In 1990, Annette married Johnnie W. Murray, Jr. (singer, musician, songwriter, producer and Grammy award winner). They have been married for thirty blessed years. Every year, they grow stronger together with their puppy, Sam I Am. Annie and John have always ministered together. They sang and played at their home churches: NJ (Bishop Joseph Scott, Jr.), PA

(Bishop Brenda Cuthbertson) or with Bishop Bruce Parham and *Praise Factor*. Before moving to Dallas, Texas in 2007, her husband led a choir, on which she sang, called *John Murray and Worship*. Annette worked in upper management for several major corporations, such as Prudential, U.S. Healthcare, Aetna and CIGNA. During her tenure at some of the major corporations, she helped open five offices for the programs that were offered by those companies. She has also traveled to train staff in Manila, Philippines.

Annette, affectionately known as Annie, was ordained, and served as a licensed Elder at the Potters House of Dallas, Texas, with Bishop T.D. Jakes under Higher Ground Organization. Annie has traveled with her husband to Brazil at least seven times to minister the gospel. She has also been to Vietnam three times to do humanitarian work. Annie currently serves alongside her husband at Northwood Church in Keller, Texas. She is an Altar Minister/Captain, Prayer Leader, Women's Ministry and much more.

Annie loves to help and serve in any way that she can. The one thing that everyone knows about Annie is that her smile brightens every room and that she is always encouraging the people she comes into contact with.

Made in the USA
Middletown, DE
17 August 2021

45470408R00051